Shopping with

Story by Jackie Tidey
Photography by Lindsay Edwards

Rigby®
A Harcourt Achieve Imprint

www.Rigby.com
1-800-531-5015

On Saturday
Anya went to Grandma's house.

Anya's mom and dad
had to go to work.

"Goodbye, Anya," said her dad.
"Have fun with Grandma."

"Anya," said Grandma,
"let's go to the store.
I have to get some food
for dinner on Sunday."

Anya and Grandma walked
all the way to the store.

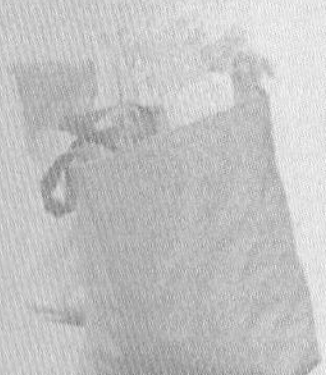

At the store
Grandma went from area to area,
and Anya helped her.

They got fish and eggs
and apples and bananas.

SALE
99

"Grandma, the shopping bags are very heavy now," said Anya.

"Yes," said Grandma, "the bags **are** very heavy. We can't walk home with all these bags."

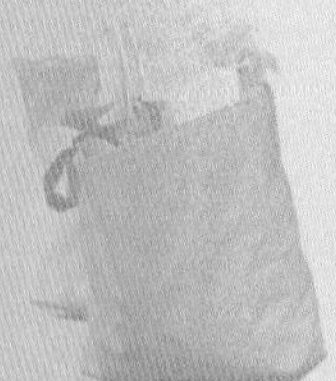

SEAFOOD
$8
$6

"Look, Grandma," said Anya.
"We can get a bag with wheels,
like that one."

"Clever girl!" said Grandma.

Anya and Grandma
looked for a bag.

Grandma got a big bag
with wheels.

ORDER NO.
STYLE NO.
COLOUR
G.W.
N.W.

“My new bag has lots of room.
We can keep shopping,” said
Grandma.

“Oh no, Grandma!”
laughed Anya.
“Can we go home now?”

"Yes," laughed Grandma,
"let's go home."